The cat flap

T0372095

Sid is looking in at Mum.
Mum gets up to let him in.

Now Sid needs to go out.
Mum gets up to let him out.

Mum feels like she lets Sid in
and out from morning to night

She is a bit sick of it.
But she has a plan.

Mum visits the pet shop
and then she gets tools
out of the shed.

She spends the morning
setting up a cat flap for Sid.

Then she is finished!

Click! Clack! Sid is out.

Click! Clack! Sid is in.

Click! Clack! Sid is out.

Click! Clack! Sid is in.

Sid purrs. Now he can
come and go as he wishes.

That night…

Click! Clack!

Sid jumps up. He sees that Miss Good's black cat Fluff is in! She is snacking on his crackers!

Sid runs at Fluff. Fluff sprints
back out. Click! Clack!

Then... Click! Clack!

Sid sits up. He smells a rat!
It is a fat rat munching on
a turnip!

Sid hurls himself at the rat. The rat is quick. He zooms off. Click! Clack!

Then...

Click! Clack!

Then...

Click! Clack!

The next morning, Mum says
to Sid, "You look worn out!
I bet you have been going
in and out all night."

"At night, I will lock your cat flap. No in and out for you!"

Thank goodness!

Words to blend

looking	Good	needs
feels	morning	for
night	tools	purrs
turnip	hurls	bends
nest	split	zooms
flops	lands	stick
wishes	milk	from

Before reading

Synopsis: Mum is tired of having to let Sid in and out, so she puts a cat flap in the door. But some others might like to come in and out too!

Review graphemes/phonemes: oo oo ee or igh ur

Story discussion: Look at the cover and read the title together. Ask: *What's happening in the cover picture? Who do you think this story is going to be about?*

Link to prior learning: Display a word with adjacent consonants from the story, e.g. *munching*. Ask children to put a dot under each single-letter grapheme (*m, u, n, i*) and a line under the digraphs (*ch, ng*). Model, if necessary, how to sound out and blend the adjacent consonants together to read the word. Repeat with another word from the story, e.g. *black*, and encourage children to sound out and blend the word independently.

Vocabulary check: turnip – a root vegetable often used in stews

Decoding practice: Ask children to turn to page 5. How quickly can they find and read the word *plan*? Check that they can blend the adjacent consonants (*pl*) together as they read.

Tricky word practice: Display the word *going*. Read the word and ask children to tell you which is the tricky bit (the *o*, which makes the sound /oa/). Look for the word in the book, and practise writing and spelling it.

After reading

Apply learning: Ask: *Why did Mum get the cat flap? Do you think her plan worked?* Check that children realise that the cat-flap plan partly worked because it meant Sid could let himself in and out. It was only a partial success, because it also meant Fluff and other animals could come into the house at night and disturb Sid's sleep.

Comprehension

- Who fitted the cat flap?

- What did Sid think of the cat flap at first?

- Why do you think Sid was glad the cat flap would be locked at night at the end of the story?

Fluency

- Pick a page that most of the group read quite easily. Ask them to reread it with pace and expression. Model how to do this if necessary.

- Encourage children to read Mum's words on page 15 with as much expression as they can.

- Practise reading the words on page 17.

Tricky words review

out	she	going
he	you	have
for	says	your
come	go	old
like	all	by